Living Diversity

Poems by

Lynn Martin

Illustrated by Karen Becker

Living Diversity

Art by Karen Becker

West Wind Words

ISBN 978-0-9852380-6-3

Table of Contents

PART ONE

The faces in the
      tenements change,
            but stay the same
poor,

yearning, as they say,
to be free

Jumping rope in Newark, New Jersey

Half opened windows to summer heat,
smack   of rope on concrete;
childhood opens with instant clarity
as if your ear is direct connection.

You remember early evenings,
sweat sweetened body
hurled into the center
expertly timing the meeting of ground
with an air-borne turning.

Everything was so simple then,
as you chanted your alphabetical
ten year old certainties.

A my name is Alice.
My husband's name is Albert
We come from Alabama
and we bring back Apples

B my name is Barbara

You had perfected even the q and the z.
Life was orderly and known.
Mother called at 8:30, Time come on home.
Father appeared at 9 to take the hand
of his chalksmelling daughter.
Grimy sneakered and growing, you reluctantly obeyed.

You hadn't a clue to life after dark,
the sheer mystery of a spinning earth
or that birth had flung you into its rhythm.
You had yet to learn
Alice acted out in senseless actions,
Albert drank and collected money
behind the bars of his eyes,
and Alabama would exist
always a day's journey away.
Apples, of course, appear and disappear
in raw moments of joy
yesterday and tomorrow.

You can hear your clear young voice
shaping the chant
as did the other children:

Alice, Albert, Barbara & me.

Crossing the George Washington Bridge

I

New York is over there; it's 1935.
I'm 3 months old; the bridge is four.

New York is not New Jersey.
True, a tenement is a tenement; a block a block.
New Jersey doesn't have 5th Avenue,
the Bowery, theaters and boroughs.
It has oceans, gardens, mountains; none of which I know about.
Kearny is just outside of Newark, and across from New York.
A Scottish town build around not wire but thread.
Looking out over the Jersey meadows
New York floats in the mist like a Camelot that was
or is about to be.

What does it mean to cross a bridge?

Now I'm seven, exiled by WW II from one state to another.
Dad moves us to Rhode Island for the duration.
Four years later we are heading back, the bridge
still there, saved by my Dad in my eleven year old opinion.
I was never quite sure what it was saved from, but
carried for the rest of my life the sense of doom
coming out of the blue and marooning us
on the wrong side of the bridge.

12 people died while building the bridge.
More than a million Americans died in WW II.
A miracle my Dad got to Africa and back.

A miracle we drove over the bridge and back to New Jersey.
Back to Kearny, Congoleum Nairn, and soccer.
I've been an exile ever since,
driving back and forth over bridges.
None of them as elegant as the George Washington.
Most of them inventions of my mind.

II

I'm working in a factory, testing linoleum.
At 17, I have no idea of anything else.
A lunchtime visitor talks of college in a near-by city.
How much I ask? And enroll.
The bridge from Kearny to Newark barely noticeable
as the bus rolls over the Passaic river.
One woman's chance remark the unseen real connection
as I do my homework between home and school.

III

What bridge do you cross to find yourself?

I stand on one side. Writers all live on the Heights across the river.
Books fall from the hands of the gods, certainly not
from those who surround me: factory workers, house cleaners.
I have to dismantle this bridge piece by piece.
Reconstruct it to my own architectural design.

Like Eliza on the ice floes,
It's one bridge after another.
Always seeking the other side.
Always dreaming of the George Washington Bridge
"the most beautiful bridge in the world",
that spider web of wires from here to there.

Misfit

Send her for a loaf of bread,
She'll bring back a lump of clay
to form the heart's perfection.

Mudspattered, grass-stained, knees
scraped and bleeding,
she never knows what time it is,
marries, cooks, rescues the children
only to walk out the door
because it is open.

The stories she tells:
Zanzibar, green buffaloes, a robin
mesmerized by its own orange dream.
She never heeds the mealtime bell,
never sees the taxicab
hellbent on business, bearing down,
so intent is she on unearthly conversation.

She doesn't even dress right.
Socks don't match, last year's blouse
is gray with age, a straw hat
tilts in an opposite direction.

Ask her to mind the store,
She'll empty the shelves
into other people's kitchens.
Down on her knees, her ear is turned
to the frogs green with singing.

Lost in her sunburned tongue
everything she touches turns to truth
she gives away   believing.

You   Sister Ruth

what you doing hiding in this store
charging twenty dollars to hold someone's hand?

Who you fooling with that turban
struggling to keep your wild hair in place?

I know you got the moon under the table
rubbing against your knee, and the sun
hiding in the cupboard, waiting.

What you doing reading palms,
taming your voice down from a lion's roar?

You think I don't remember
that night in North Carolina
when the hills were touched with fire
and every pond was black with ice,

you dancing the blaze into ash,
sliding over the water with bare feet
kicking the surface into shards
that sang like small bells in my ears,

or when you poled a flatbottomed boat
over the Louisiana flood, pulling tiny animals
from the water to toss at your feet,
their fur, matted like wet dishrags, piled high
accepting your saving hand; that resurrection
was your business and the order of the day?

8

Now what you doing here in Philadelphia
surrounded by variety stores,

the El shaking plate glass windows,
causing futures to rumble in your hand?

Why search a guru

Why search a guru in a desert waste,
top of mountain, empty space.

Use but a mirror clear,
look within without fear.

What you see is all you need,
you are the humble mustard seed.

Not someone who stands without,
within is what it's all about.

Toni

I dream a world
you get it all down   such a hard world
me in it learning
what it is to be black
in the usa   what it is to be white
in the usa   both   or nothing
makes sense   you are not left out
you went all the way up to the bottom
can it possibly be true

You said there is no America
without sula nell macon judas
they are all here forever
have always been here
I know you didn't write them
for me but a world in a book
is everyone's and once read
becomes my world and so
I want to run out and let
a hundred balloons loose
race through the town shouting
way to go Toni
oh **girl girl girl**

PART TWO

In joy beneath the sky
As down the roadway
Passing boys and girls
Go singing too,
In time of silver rain
   When spring
   And life
   Are new.

Langston Hughes

Silence in the Snowy Woods

A great swoop over my head, and a steady beat of wings. Suddenly a dark shape banks, turns and disappears into the pines. I had startled an owl into flight. It happened too quickly for me to do more than sense a shadow against the sky, as if the spirit of the pine trees had broken off a piece of darkness to carry even deeper into the woods. Owls do seem to open into mystery, and this one, in the silence it left behind, seemed to call. I vaguely began to follow where I thought it had flown, knowing I'd probably not see it again. Owls are hard to spot by an amateur like me. This is the first one I'd seen in six months of living here. Yet I knew it lived close by. I heard its hoots from my bedroom window late at night. I walked deeper into the snowy woods, daylight having lingered long enough to leave some light, or was it only a snow gathered glow? I stopped. Silence. Nothing moved. Nothing, except myself, seemed to breath. Remarkable, since I knew the woods held sleeping birds, barely awakened rabbits, curled up moles, deer, turkeys, and grouse. Certainly porcupines and raccoons. The sense of a complete world I couldn't see filled the night air. The owl, I felt, was somewhere. Watching.

I do seem to wander in directions marked by vaguely perceived movement. Logic and goals are not my strong suit. I can't explain any of my life in logic's strict terms. Why do I go here? Why did I do that? There seems no reason other than because I did. Like Roethke:

"I wake to sleep, and take my waking slow.
I feel my fate in what I cannot fear.
I learn my going where I have to go."

The little boy Welcome House Adoption Agency put into my arms so many years ago. What logic brought us together? A six month old, brown all over, as if just in from the beach, black silky hair framing a solemn face dominated by huge blue eyes. I can still hear Pearl Buck's voice somewhere over my head saying, "Isn't he beautiful? Is he Polynesian?" I could understand why she would say that. I am sure he was lifted from a canoe found floating down a river which emptied into the heart of Philadelphia, this Moses child who was now to be my son. My first born son. Such miracles are not planned. My journey to this place was as subject to currents and wind as the path of this child. No, he wasn't Polynesian. He was Filipino and born in Philadelphia. No matter. His hair smelled of salt splashed bark.

My next son arrived via my birth canal. Not content with canoes, he chartered a non-stop Queen Elizabeth, landing at my feet carrying chunks of sea-weed and the light of a new moon in his face. Maybe he didn't get here first, but his cry would insure no second-hand attention. He was a presence not to be ignored. What was this assurance he carried in his tiny hands? Where could he have been before he decided to enter my life? Wherever it was he knew how to talk to trees, to wander comet-colliding skies without fear, to ask questions no mere mother could answer.

When the two boys were seven and eight, wherefore came the stray thought a daughter would be wonderful, a completion of a circle that existed somewhere inside myself. And so a warrior

17

daughter arrived whose ancestors walked an African landscape, and whose brown eyes still held the glow. She screamed the walls into out-of-plumb shape in a small room in Hackensack, New Jersey where I met her for the first time. As I held her, she hiccupped small wet sobs into the nape of my neck. This softness in contrast to her former fury won me forever. Someone had to soothe her outrage. We had both found our way to the Jersey meadows, sharp grass notwithstanding, to a city neither of us had ever been in before and might never visit again.

I was deep into the woods now. Night had used up all the remaining light. If the owl was there I wouldn't be able to see it even if it were right in front of me. I was growing older. My children were grown. What would the remaining part of my life hold? I turned and began to follow my own footprints out of the woods. What a wandering way I had come. Barely a straight line anywhere. In and out of trees, around clumps of tangled branches, a long trek over a mound of rocks. Could this really be the way I'd come? I'd just have to keep going and find out.

On the day my firstborn son arrived

There were no balloons
only a wind that blew the ocean
into a pleated skirt of promise,
blue as your eyes; the sun
a saffron ball barely seen
through clouds in a hurry to arrive.

Driving through Pennsylvania Dutch country
farms rich with barns flashed by,
each protected by a hex sign meant
to keep demons from the door.
How would I protect you
with your dark, curly hair and unknown

Filipino grandparents preparing a boat
this early morning to put out to sea,
fish lines curled under their toes
as they had done forever, while your new,
white parents take you in their arms, feel

your six month old body relax.
Taking you home, we stare at the blurred
landscape, lulled by the rhythm of the car
the sound of our own hearts beating.

Adoption

Testing the world
the new kitten
challenges rugs,
each ray of light,
the direction of warmth.

Like you
when you arrived
protesting loudly
the new arms against your skin,

and like the kitten
trust was a slow process
a luring from under the bed,
careful movements until another's hands
were proven to be without harm.

You were too little for words
had been passed from house to house,
the soles of your feet already tough,
each curl on your head
tightly wound and bristling.

You had no choice
but to take what was
taste and touch everything in the house
making it familiar until it was yours:
a crib, a teddy bear, a mother.

The way it is

Think of the hair on their sweet heads.
One black as the eye of midnight,
soft to the touch, without curl.
Another blond, scruffy with impossible demands.
The youngest tightly wound and bristling.
Two boys and a girl. An American mix.

And think of the points of arrival.
Bucks County with acres of rich farms
as far from the Philippines as anyone can imagine,
and yet, here is my first born transferred from
Pearl Buck's arms to my own.
Second son is pushed out from my own body,
surprised by the brother already in residence.
Their sister, years later, football shouldered,
African songed: a family.

While nations divide one race from another,
three children call each other brother, sister.
Their questing eyes do not ask the rightness
of this. Children learn what they see.

I hear their laughter as they discover
the pond down the road, the mystery
of apple trees whose limbs invite like ladders,
hay stacked for hiding and finding. Years
later I ask second son if he would have preferred
to be an only child. He doesn't deign to answer,
only searches out his older brother who is teasing

his sister, and inserts himself between them.
His hand reaches out to them,
seeking comfort in the known.

PART THREE

Someone, I tell you,
will remember us.

Sappho

Michael In Winter

As soon as the roads are clear, there is Michael
pumping past my window, one hand waving

as if he knows I'm watching. He believes
in the magic of numbers: two arms, two legs,

two wheels on his bicycle. It is his only
possession, and he rides, awkward body

hunched over handlebars, front wheel weaving
along our country roads, totally ignoring passing cars.

Michael in winter is slow movement
making circles from miles of highway,

believing in his orange cap, that it protects
him from strangers who drive past, blurred

and grumbling at this boy-man in their path.
I, stiff seated in the glow of my computer,

circle the poem I'm trying to write, juggling
the awkward body of words, oblivious

to cold winter hills leaning on my windowsill.
I have never met Michael

but we both love bicycles, mumble chants
based on numbers, wander on uncertain wheels.

Come down Isaiah

Twined round a branch like an airborne root,
       the boy looks down from three branches up.

He is not about to descend.
       Certainly not to this white woman's command.

She thinks he will fall.
       He looks down on her with disdain,

continues to climb & climb & climb.
       Isaiah is five years old and already he knows

the only way is up.

The apple tree   stands alone

having survived the renovations
on the surrounding apartments.

Stands alone

in this little Vermont suburbia
of low income housing.

Stands alone

among the many-hued children
who find its twisted branches irresistible.
They perch like birds at every level
chattering, laughing, shouting pure nonsense,
imagining themselves a multitude of fairy tale lives.
When the children leave, real birds descend.
Chickadee, Purple finch, Cardinal,
Jay, Crow, Sparrow, Goldfinch.
They add their calls to the day.
The Cardinal vibrates red,
the finch gilds itself into song.
Then one night in Spring
white, like snow, takes over,
whole blossoms, pink tinged, crowd the air,
until wind steals each one
littering the grass, the walk, my car,
that little one's hair.

Shorn of blossoms, the apple tree

stands alone
                waiting.

Freewheelin' Teens

They come on wheels,
young faces fierce with intention.
The way they hold their heads,
shouts, I am the best
or if not I will be
as time after time they
approach the wall
and by some trick of gravity
are atop it, skateboard and all,
racing to the end
and down again
as easy as landing a spaceship
in the moonlight,   Then they
tip forward to an instant stop,
and grin.

Caught

Eyes round, scared
skinny body rigid, hands clenched
to ward off whatever is
about to come.   He
stands defiant after spearing
my garbage can and wiping
my steps clear of flowers.

He's caught red handed
but no
"I didn't do anything"
he hurls through gritted teeth.

He did, but why quibble.
He's seven year old
and had been deep in slaying dragons.
Was it his fault one had wandered
to my porch?
"It won't happen again, will it?" I ask
this little knight.
No, he pledges
and I believe him.
"I dub you protector of my porch," I say
and hope for the best.

Sorcery

for Tashiko Takaezu

Blue with the world
she rushes to get it right
to get it down the only way possible
and so the circles rise,
roll out the door,
huge clay bowls
without beginning or end.

It's a fever, yes
a promise of almost perfection,
a world where blue
begins to glow orange
for here everywhere is herself,
a brand new being to hold in her hands.
This tiny woman consumed by creation
repeats the internal roundness
we all need to hear.

Her own name is a whisper: Tashiko.
She builds a bigger kiln
and it's never large enough
to capture whatever it is
that prowls outside of the white heat
she stokes higher and higher
until gaining momentum
even death for a while
hums at the door.

The ordinary enters her soul.
Life begins in the sorcerer's lair.
There on the wheel
out of the earth itself
a new form
like a prayer for us all.

Revelation

It was on National Public Radio
He called him Grandpa.

Can you imagine Gandhi
not only a man in a loincloth
freeing India from English rule
talking of God, but

a grandfather who held a young man's hand,
maybe even had to bandage a skinned knee

maybe even frowned?

Born in Africa

Yes, there he is.
Singing! On stage !

Can you believe it?

Born in Africa, he sings.
He who will die
in a few months time.

Look at his face
honed to the bone at thirty-eight,

his feet ulcerated and washed
by a lone Samaritan
while others turn away.

Where does he get his strength
to ride the length and breadth of
Uganda?

Yes, there he is.
Singing alone and frightened
of living with AIDS.

Shining forth in remote villages.
Walking the streets of Kampala in
pain.

Rising into the hot wind of Africa.
This son of heaven,
this Philly Lataaya,

this man who sings for us all.

On the hospital lawn

a lament for all the children who have died of AIDS

None of us were there
that day. A butterfly,
a thousand miles of travel in its wings,
kept watch, a flutter
of orange above the just clipped green.

Above the just clipped green,
a mother holds a child to the sun,
the baby's heart a flutter,
now unfurled, now retracted,
now gone.

Now gone,
above the just clipped green,
where the sun
is snagged by cloud,
and hidden.

The baby in her mother's arms,
with the doctor's blessing,
taken from the hospital halls,
out into an orange dream,
to die against her mother's breast.

Out into an orange dream,
above the just clipped green.
None of us were there that day,

where the sun, snagged by cloud,
lay hidden. The baby's heart
a flutter, now unfurled,
now retracted,   gone

Blood ties

One

At ten, they pricked my finger.
I wasn't, like Sleeping Beauty
lulled to sleep.

It hurt. A rose, so tiny
they whisked it away, exploded.

Anemic, said the doctor.

I was afraid this brightness from within
was forever lost.

At fourteen, I bled again,
from a different place.

There was no doctor,
and, so, I was safe.
Do you remember growing up?

Two

The chart is flat.
A human outline is a black line.
All the veins are red,
traveling from the heart
to the fingertips, the toes, the brain.

So simple,
the heart pumps,

oxygen reaches my furthermost cell
I am alive!

In fifth grade,   I know enough
not to leap up, search behind the figure.

What tells a heart to begin?
What is love and its absence?

Why does it stop?

Three

I was positive I would
continue to love the woods
behind the playground.

In a city, not far from Newark,
stretched taut along the Hudson River,

separated from New York City by muskrats,
feral cats, an infinity of water,

I was positive I would find love.
So, I did.

The beat of my heart stopped my ears,
even though our body's fluid
flowed behind latex dams.
You are positive in a different way.

I love you. You, with your hand in mine,
me, with my hand in yours.

How many miracles can we ask for?

<u>Four</u>

Blood bank, blood brother, blood cell, blood count,
blood group, blood-line, blood pressure, blood-red.

**a plant of the poppy family
having a red root and sap and bearing
a solitary lobed leaf and a white flower
in early spring**

blood-stock, blood-stone, blood-stream,
a mainstream of power or vitality.

Blood ties. I tell you, in this life all we have is each other.

Hawking Condoms

Today I met with the people of "Sojourner House".
Me, this woman
who comes with a story of saving lives.
They've heard it before.

They talk and talk and talk.
I listen and listen and turn my ear desperately closer.
They are polite, look out windows, down at the floor,
toward the door.

Polite they crowd me at the table. It's their lives.

"I've been poisoned by lead. The doctors don't know.
I'm sick. I'm toxic. The same as AIDS."
"Afraid. I'm afraid. I'm afraid of the rain. "That's William.
"Do you know about AIDS?" I ask.
"Water will eat the buttons off my shirt," he replies.

Steve talks of Hartford hustlers, "clean, they are clean
Tested every six months and no need for rubbers."
He's here, small towning it, hiding from heroin.
Tells me of cutting, pure percentages,
his woman and selling; the black woman whose kid
he took care of while he was on the lam.
And Mary's out there with her johns. "She's got
the Thing. That's what they say, she's got the Thing."
"The whole world's poison, don't you know. The doctors
they don't care."

Sha-an, Asian refugee, insists he was born
here in New England
struggling with English to plead,
"some things you just don't talk about."
He's in agony, sneaking looks at gold foil circles
ringing the table. Then he's gone.
Bolted. Melted. Out the door.

"Poison.   Poison." is shouted at Annie learning
to write her name.
Over the A painstakingly rising from her broken crayon,
She chooses a bright blue condom
to wear in her hair.

The Strange Ones

They walk the roads
  to and from town over and over.

They sit in the library
  from the time it opens until it closes.

They patrol the post office
  brandishing a scroll of unintelligible protests.

They proclaim the end of the world.
  They are the strange ones.

And then I look in the mirror.

Even Napoleon had a place to go

Once upon a time in nineteen forty-one
a father joined the United States navy.
Home disappeared
into an endless ride to Mom's parents
in another world.
Best friends left behind,
known paths to school, to the playground
disappeared. Alone I walked
into a classroom with hieroglyphics
written in chalk on a blackboard.
My first grade printing
not up to a cursive second grade.

A child follows her parents without question.
A father off to war leaves an always anxious
why?

I can't imagine
an endless trek,
whole cities blown into dust
behind.
Everything possible put in your path
to prevent going anywhere .
Best friends missing or dead.
Nowhere to go. No second grade
even if the language is illegible.

Exile to somewhere,
a country, an island, a place.
All anyone is looking for is
home.

Coming out

We all wander in somehow
like battlescarred waifs
tearstreaked eyes awed open

and there we are on the midway.

Six feet high lights blind us.
A merry-go-round with lavender steeds shouts.

From under a hot sun,
longskirted Sappho winks.
and isn't that Radcliffe: serious face
solemn, no longer lonely.

Now the cottoncandy lady tempts.
None of us resist,
digging into grubby jeans for whatever it is
we have to offer.

Bang goes the cannon.
Our favorite gym teacher dives into sky
painted above our upturned heads
in one long drawn out needy O.

We almost ask where we are,
but this is rebirth, so there's nothing to do but turn
the gift of lollypop over in our mouths
as we tumble to be first in line

for bumper cars, loop the loop,   fortuneteller.
Satiated, we warm sticky hands on the rising sun,
seek any bed available, nose down onto silken sheets.
Paradise, like confetti, settles on our hair.

Babydyke Rapper

Jeans half way down my ass.
T-shirt belly button short.

A slide between Butch and Fem
that's my style. Keep em guessing.

Eye shadow, lipstick, shaved head,
eyebrow pierced with a glint of gold.

Les, Bi, Trans? Who knows?
Don't ask. Don't tell.

I write. I sing. I draw.

I ask Jonathon to the movies.
Jennifer to the dance,

both to the peace march
on the other side of town.

What's my coming out story?
Hell, I was born out.

My first sound was a growl.

Now I'm me,
somewhere between Susan B and Malcolm X.

Someday I'll vote

I'm a babydyke rapper

I'm twelve

I'm me

I'm here

The Other Country

"I wish there were somewhere
actual we could stand."

Adrienne Rich

Dawn is spreading out, a gradual advance,
a taking in of mountains, the red
turning of a maple lead, a distance
of fields. This slow awakening where the head
turns on the pillow, eyes are open
and staring, the breath steady and sure.

In the other country
the harvest passes though hands
the color of earth, or maybe
a shadow of saffron from the underside
of a wing. A matter
of an early morning in fall where color
is a celebration, a dance, a song of joy.

In the other country, people aren't afraid
to laugh, a soaring over rivers
like swallows stitching the air into day.
The child is running to school
with a shiny yellow cap, swinging
a full lunch pail that catches the sun
in its handle, full of laughter in the new day.

Yes, Wendell, I am on my way

I will secede
from the government of money and war
from the government of division
from a fear of oneself translating into a fear of the other
I ask everyone to hold with Mr. Berry
in the open farmland, the deepest woods
the highest mountains, the quietest lakes
Yes, yes, I will hold fast against a river of money
designed to benefit only the rich
I will call everyone neighbor, call and call all people
to stand beneath the stars that belong to everyone.

Acknowledgments

Special thanks to Anne Alexander whose skills made this book possible and to Matthew Wojcik and Jeanne Walsh at the Brooks Memorial Library. I am grateful for the continual support and encouragement of Linda and Graham Gordon, Marguerite Monet, Louise Radar and, as always, my daughter Tarn Martin.